Your Weekly Guide to Bliss

52 Ways to Welcome Happiness and Cultivate a Life You Love

Ginger Marie Corwin

Your Weekly Guide to Bliss: 52 Ways to Welcome Happiness and Cultivate a Life You Love

1952 Annandale Way
Pomona, CA 91767

Visit the author's website at lifecoachgingermarie.com

ISBN: 9781520973609

Editing by Dana Johnson.

Cover by Ben Knight. Used with permission.

Dedication

I dedicate this book to my parents, Ray and Charlotte Koesel, and my future husband, Nic Corwin. Thank you for your unconditional love and support. You have always been my #1 fans and made me believe that I could be and do anything. I love you!

I also dedicate this book to my biological father, Joseph Koesel. You are one reason I felt so determined to change my life and make happiness and self-love a priority. Your story and memory inspires me to help other people find happiness in their own lives.

Contents

Preface

Let me begin by taking a moment to introduce myself. My name is Ginger Marie Corwin. I am a Life Coach, Angel Card Reader, Yogi, and Author. Wow, it feels amazing to write those words, especially *author*. Until recently, I would never have guessed I would add that line of work to my completed bucket list.

I know I am being called to write this book. As I sit down to write these words I am not completely sure of all that will come through, but I am trusting the process. I have faith that I am being guided.

Having faith is something that I have become rather good at. It is a work in progress, but I am a whole lot better at practicing it than I've ever been. The idea of writing this book began with many divinely orchestrated signs and synchronicities. Over the past few weeks I have seen or heard many signs that have led me to this moment.

First, I started pulling angel cards (similar to tarot cards, but they use only positive images and words) that said *author* or *writing*. Next, I received an email message asking me to volunteer for a book-writing event in Vegas. I started seeing many Facebook ads about becoming an author and writing a book. I heard "Start writing" in many meditations as the answer to my prayers. I was watching one of my favorite spiritual teachers on YouTube, and the premise of her message was writing her first book. Lastly, I was watching the revival of *Gilmore Girls*, where Rory finally decides to write her own book based on her life and relationship with her mother.

These next three synchronicities are what finally convinced me to act on this guidance.

Although I felt I was being guided to write, I was also experiencing a lot of fear and resistance. I prayed on it and asked for support. A few days later, I was on Facebook and saw an ad for a beta-testing group for people who want to write and self-publish their first book. I applied. I thought this would be a perfect way to be both supported and held accountable, which I clearly needed. A few days later, I received an email message stating I was accepted into the group program, free of charge.

That same week, I attended a large speaking event. While there, I saw a gentleman and intuitively heard, "Speak to him. He will be able to help you." I found this weird as I knew nothing about this man and felt awkward approaching him.

The next day, I saw this gentleman during a break, and I found the nerve to speak with him. While making small talk, he told me about the Amazon best-selling book he had self-published. Immediately I knew what my intuition was telling me and how he would be able to help. I mentioned to him that I was starting to write my own book and was feeling a little lost and overwhelmed.

The day after the event he emailed me. I was planning to email him that same day and laughed at the coincidence. Later, during our call, I took over four pages of notes of his guidance on how to write, market, and publish my book. He also offered to review my work and help keep me accountable during this process.

The following week, a best-selling Amazon author and business coach was offering a scholarship for her 90-day group program on book writing. To win the scholarship, we candidates had to listen to her daily Facebook live videos and comment with our key takeaways. At the end of the week, we had to answer a series of questions. I had a strong inclination all week that I was going to win.

On the day of the drawing, she announced there would be three levels of scholarship winners. One winner would receive a $500 scholarship, another would receive a $1000 scholarship, and the last winner would receive the program free of charge.

Guess who that person was...ME! I was thrilled. I had just received a $2,250 scholarship for a program that was going to teach me how to write and self-publish my book.

The Universe brought the people and resources I needed to make my dream a reality. As Wayne Dyer once said, "If prayer is you talking to God, then intuition is God talking to you." Well, God was talking directly to me. (Understand that in this book I will use the words *God* and *Universe* interchangeably. To me they are the same, called by many names. I encourage you to use whatever name resonates with you.)

Some of you may be thinking these are coincidences. I don't believe in coincidences. As I have begun to understand life's magic and winks from the Universe, I now realize what we may think is coincidental is the Universe's attempt to bring us what we want. As Albert Einstein is often credited for saying, "Coincidence is God's way of remaining anonymous."

I believe we are always being led, but not everyone chooses to pay attention or follow the guidance they receive. I found that the "how" of bringing this book into being slowly began to reveal itself to me as I surrendered and began letting go of controlling how I was going to make it happen.

As the signs kept coming, I admit that I experienced resistance a few times. Heck, it took me about a month from the first sign to sit down and write. But here it goes.

Whether you realize it or not, you are also being guided. There is a reason you picked up or were given this book, and I am honored that our paths have crossed.

My intention is for my words to speak directly to you, into your heart. I hope that in some way my work helps to make your life flow better and your light shine brighter. I also hope that you feel more inspired and guided to follow your bliss.

My Story

As I mentioned earlier, this author thing is new to me, but it is a natural extension from my life's work. As a life coach, I help women who are searching for a deeper level of happiness and self-love to find self-acceptance, power in their thoughts, and happiness in the present moment, so they can feel financially free, fiercely confident, and in control of their lives.

Through the long and extensive search to find myself, I have discovered that one purpose I have on this earth is to be of service, to help others find happiness and self-love within themselves.

This is important to me for many reasons, the first being it took me a long time to find happiness and self-love. Honestly, it is something that I continue to work on. I do not feel that happiness and self-love are something that you achieve once and then you're set forever; it is something that you work on every single day. Just as you establish and maintain any kind of relationship, being happy and in love with yourself requires continual attention because you grow and evolve. The second reason why it is important for me to help others involves my family, and I will get more into that shortly.

To understand fully the growth that I have experienced in my own adult life, you need to have a picture of what my life was like before.

I was in my mid-twenties and had gone through a pretty hard few years. I was passed up for four different promotions at work, each one more painful than the last. I saw my friends and peers making more money and accepting higher positions while I couldn't get a promotion to save my life. With each rejection, I would ask for feedback, and the common response I received was that I did not have "executive presence." I didn't know it at the time, but your vibration, or vibe, speaks louder than your words. And I was putting out some pretty stinky vibes.

I was unhappy in my job. I would cry on my way home from work almost every day. My friends would always try to cheer me up, and I constantly felt bad that I was dampening their day with my tears. Some of them even seemed to be distancing themselves or avoiding me altogether. Truthfully, I was not very much fun to be around at the time.

I needed clarity on where I wanted my life to go. I thought that I had finally figured it all out when I realized I had a love for event planning. I took a significant pay decrease and left my job to go to another company working in event productions. It ended up not being what I expected, and I disliked the job even more than my last, which I believed at the time was impossible. I thought being unemployed would be better than the situation I had found myself in, so I resigned after two months. I was unemployed for several weeks before I decided to go back to my old company, feeling like a failure.

The hard times I experienced between companies evoked a serious scarcity mindset. I was afraid of not having enough money. I was barely scraping by in one of the most expensive cities in the country, Los Angeles.

My dating life was not what I wanted it to be. It seemed that every man I dated was emotionally unavailable or not looking for a relationship. I dated man after man, none looking to settle down. The relationship would end, and I would feel alone and abandoned, which became a story I perpetually created for myself for many years. The last guy I dated broke up with me over the phone a week before taking me home for Thanksgiving to meet his family. I was devastated and convinced something was wrong with me. I started drinking more wine than was wise and found partying a good way to numb what I was feeling.

I was not confident in myself and was always playing the comparison game. I made other people more special in my mind or would try to tear them down to make myself feel better. I was constantly a victim of my own negative self-talk and criticism.

I was unhappy. I remember wanting more out of life and thinking there had to be a better way. In fact, I vividly recall a conversation with my mother where I asked, "How can I be happy now? What is the secret to being happy?"

I went to a therapist to try to find clarity and answers. After explaining how I was feeling, my therapist said a few words that would forever change my life: "I think you're depressed." I left her office that day, replaying her words repeatedly in my head.

The reason her words stuck with me so strongly is because of my past, which I mentioned earlier I would touch on again. When I was a few months old, I was put in the care of my aunt and uncle, whom I consider my parents and who later raised me. Both my biological parents suffered from mental illness. My dad had paranoid schizophrenia and was an addict, and my mom had manic depression. My whole life I grew up with the fear that I too would live a similar fate and suffer from depression or a form of mental illness.

That day in the therapist office something shifted within me. I resolved at that moment my fate would not be depression. I decided that getting by each day was not good enough anymore. I made a promise to myself that I was going to be happy and, not only that, I *deserved* to be happy.

With the decision made, I transformed my life for the better. I started seeing a life coach named Meg Haines. I had met her at an event months earlier, and her work intrigued me. I had been on her email list for many months but had never taken action. It was something I thought about doing and knew would be good for me but experienced resistance and fear around the thought of signing up.

One day in January of 2015, I received one of her newsletters and something inside of me lit up and beckoned me to reach out. *Thank you, Angels!* I was willing to change, and my choosing happiness is what allowed divine intervention. You see, we all have free will, and often our angels and guides will not interfere unless we ask for help. My declaration was just that—a call for help. Oh, did they answer!

After I began working with Meg, the changes started immediately. With the right mindset and attitude, the results were incredible! I remember my second call with Meg. I had taken all her suggestions and recommendations and run with them. She was blown away by the work that I had done in such a short time.

I read tons of self-help books, some of the most influential being *You Can Heal Your Life* by Louise Hay, *Loveability: Knowing How to Love and Be Loved* by Robert Holden, and *Love is Letting Go of Fear* by Gerald Jampolsky, all of which I constantly recommend to my clients and community.

Understanding that my thoughts created my reality completely changed my life. I began to be deliberate with my thoughts and, in turn, every major aspect of my life changed.

By intentionally noticing my thoughts and thinking positively, I shifted my perception of the world and learned to love myself more deeply. I strengthened my relationships with those around me; I began to change limited beliefs about money; and I stopped using phrases like "not worthy," "can't afford," and "don't deserve."

After six months of deepening my own self-love, I met my amazing fiancé, Nic. With him, I have found a more profound love than I had ever experienced or had even thought possible. I landed my dream job as an event planner and doubled my income over the previous year. I found an ocean-view apartment blocks away from the beach in Venice, California. I noticed how people began to interact with me more positively, and I started attracting more abundance into my life, including more money, trips, and prizes. The best part was I genuinely felt happy, and it radiated out of me to everyone around me.

It was during this year of unbelievable growth that I realized I wanted to be a life coach to help other women feel what I was feeling. I was driving in the car to work listening to a video by Oprah Winfrey, and I started to cry. It was in this moment that I experienced clarity. I wanted to be a coach. I heard it so clearly and felt it so deeply.

Having had a few members of my family struggle with depression and other illnesses, I saw firsthand how happiness, or a lack thereof, can change someone's life. I was ready to change lives just as I had changed my own.

Similar to how I feel guided to write this book, I felt guided to start a coaching business. I took it day by day, and the path and resources came to me to make it happen. I began building social-media sites; created my website, lifecoachgingermarie.com; hired two business coaches; attended trainings; and began building my business. A few months later, I left my full-time job and dived head first into my coaching business.

A month after I set out on my own, I enrolled in 200 hours of yoga teacher training. I had always wanted to receive my yoga certification because one of my long-term goals is to host retreats that incorporate both life coaching and yoga.

On my vision board, I had placed a photo of a yoga certificate, with my name on it, issued from the studio where I practiced. (If you are unfamiliar with a vision board, it is a collection of photos and words that depict the life you want to create.) Soon after, I received an email that my studio was awarding scholarships for training, and I applied. I was not surprised in the slightest when I received an email less than 24 hours later saying I was awarded 50 percent off my tuition. Another example of how the Universe was conspiring with me to make my dreams a reality.

I believe that I was put on this earth to help others improve their mind, body, and spirit. I hope my story shows you that anything is possible. You can create the life that you desire, and when you have faith and trust, the Universe will help you make it happen.

Introduction

During my own happiness journey, I was coached on, read about, and researched being happy. The techniques I used helped change my life, and I wanted to share them to help others change their lives as well.

During my first year as a life coach, I had an inspired idea of creating the My Weekly Bliss Challenge. Each Sunday I put out a challenge, which focused on creating bliss in your life. For one year, I challenged my community to take time every day to focus on their own happiness.

After a full year of these challenges, I felt the urge to share them in a bigger way. With sensing the internal nudge to write a book, I took it as the perfect opportunity to compile my challenges. These are tools and techniques that I have practiced to help myself and the clients I coach to create lives that we love.

This book is a collection of 52 challenges that bring more happiness, self-love, positivity, gratitude, and self-care into your life. Each challenge is followed by questions to consider to use active thinking to maximize your results of the challenge. It is important to take the time to reflect and answer each question for yourself as they are designed to help you understand who you are, what you want, and how to get it.

The book is laid out with the intention of completing one challenge a week for one year. You can begin at any time in the year. I encourage you to start a challenge on the same day every week, such as each Sunday, and make reading the challenge a part of your routine.

Each week you take on the challenge and incorporate it into your life as I suggest or in another way that feels authentic to you. I have created a Facebook group called "I Choose Bliss," where you can share your experiences and ask any questions you may have as you live out the challenges. The link to my Facebook group is www.facebook.com/groups/ichoosebliss.

I want you to use these challenges in a way that makes sense to you. If you do not want to do one challenge a week, maybe do one challenge a day or simply open a page and do the challenge you are called to do. However you decide to use these challenges, I hope they fill your life with happiness.

If you can relate at all to my story, I feel for you. My intention is to help you realize that happiness is a choice. By changing your thoughts, you can change your life. I wish that I had known this small nugget years ago. Once I did, I transformed my life.

You can transform your life, too. I know that you are ready because have this book in your hand. The first step is being willing to change. If you are willing, now is the perfect time to get started.

But first, let me share a few important things with you about happiness…

What You Need to Know About Happiness

So, what exactly is happiness?

Dictionary.com says that happiness is "the quality or state of being happy" or "good fortune; pleasure; contentment; joy."[1]

Happiness can mean many things to many different people. What brings one person joy does not necessarily bring another person joy. This book is about you discovering what brings *you* joy through a collection of tools and resources. The idea is that you should commit to doing more of whatever brings you feelings of pleasure, contentment, and joy.

Before starting your first challenge, there are a few more things you should know about happiness.

You Resist Your Own Happiness

One of the main functions of your brain is to keep you safe. Recent neuroscience research shows that the brain is resistant to change and will try to protect you from change.[2] When you set a goal or strive to make changes that require significant thought-pattern or behavioral changes, you will resist. Your brain will do whatever it takes to avoid pain, discomfort, and fear. If you have fear of failure, the brain will try to return to what it knows—that is, to its comfortable and familiar behavior and thinking patterns, even if they are harmful.

You may experience this when you are wanting to make positive changes in your life such as cultivating a deeper level of happiness just as if you were going after any other big goal or dream. When you are about to step out of your comfort zone or do something your brain sees as risky, it will go into protection mode.

To remain safe, you may even resist your own happiness or doing the things that make you happy. For instance, I am sure that you have heard that working out and eating healthy is good for you, but you may be resistant to doing it. You may know that being outside brightens up your day, but you may be resistant to making time in your day to do it.

Although you were equipped to resist change, you can overcome this obstacle by acknowledging your fear and recognizing your behavior. Continue to imagine your goals and visualize what you want. Know that it is possible for you. Repeatedly think about your overall goal to light you up and inspire you, then act to make it happen. Even baby steps are steps in the right direction.

I am sharing this with you so can come fully prepared to meet each challenge. You *will* feel resistance to these positive changes. Your mind will try to convince you it is easier or safer to stay where you are. In these moments, I encourage you to reflect on why you made the decision to read this book. Do you feel lost after a recent breakup? Do you feel like something is missing in your life? Do you have a big goal and need help achieving it? Do you want to change your mindset?

Whatever the reason, I will help you. The tools gathered in this book will help you. You must be ready and willing to push forward and commit to taking action despite the resistance you may feel. Remember, you have me and an entire Facebook community of people who are just like you, trying to make the same changes. Reach out for support as needed at facebook.com/groups/ichoosebliss.

You Do Not Need to Search for Happiness

I often hear my clients use wording such as "I want to find happiness," "I am looking for happiness in my life," or "I am searching for a deeper level of happiness."

Do any of these sentences resonate with you and describe your current mindset? If so, I have good news for you! Happiness is not a destination you need to find. Happiness is here. You do not search for or find it. You create it.

Searching for happiness has future implications. It sounds like something you will arrive at down the road. It also sounds as though you are looking for happiness outside of yourself or that you are giving your happiness away to outside people or circumstances.

You have the right to be happy at any given moment, and you can be. The challenges in this book will help you learn how to be.

You Do Not Have to Wait for Happiness

Do any of the phrases below sound familiar to you?

I will be happy when…

- I am financially free
- I am making money doing what I love
- I have a successful business
- I retire
- I no longer need a job
- I move to my dream house
- I meet "the one"
- I fall madly in love
- I have a family
- I have a super fit body
- a long list of things get checked off.

Or, I am happy now, but I will be even happier when…

So, when exactly will those things happen? Next week? Three months from now? A year from now? Twenty years from now?

What if the circumstances or events you are waiting for don't happen at the rate you want them to, or even at all? *Are you still okay waiting to be happy?*

As noted in Robert Holden's book *Be Happy: Release the Power of Happiness in YOU*, "Most researchers agree that over the long term, life circumstances influence happiness levels by 10 percent at most."[3] This means that if you are waiting for financial freedom, a successful business, your soulmate, and so on, and you are not happy before these circumstances happen, you will most likely not be much happier after these circumstances happen.

To live a truly happy life, you need to find a way to be happy despite your current circumstances. You need to be happy before you create financial freedom, build a successful business, meet your soulmate, and so on.

Every thought is made up of energy and vibrates at a particular frequency. Positive thoughts such as peace, happiness, joy, and acceptance vibrate at a high frequency and, in turn, attract positive events and circumstances through the law of attraction.

Negative thoughts such as anger, fear, guilt, or shame, vibrate at a low frequency and, in turn, produce negative events and circumstances. If you want to change your outcome, focus on changing your thoughts to positive ones, and then your circumstances will change also. Like attracts like. You will attract what you *predominantly* think about.

Now that you know and understand a little more about happiness, it is time to welcome your happiness and begin your first challenge. I know that you are ready. Let's begin.

Week One:

Decide to Be Happy the Moment You Wake Up

"Most folks are about as happy as they make up their minds to be."
—Unknown; often attributed to Abraham Lincoln

Decide to Be Happy the Moment You Wake Up

Often, your first few thoughts and experiences in the morning will determine how your day will unfold. Say, for instance, that you wake up and stub your toe or notice an unpleasant email in your inbox. If you are not deliberate with and aware of your thoughts, this rough start could potentially dampen or even ruin your day.

With practice, you can learn to control your thoughts and make the choice to be happy. Once I became aware of and began being deliberate with my thoughts in the morning, I saw a drastic change. The days when I intentionally made the decision to be happy were often higher on the happiness scale than the days when I did not wake up with the same mindset.

So, if happiness is a choice, don't you *want* to be happy?

Well, you can be! When you wake up each morning this coming week, decide that you are happy and that today is a good day! Affirm, "I choose how I feel today and I choose to be happy!" Repeat this affirmation out loud or in your head for a few minutes and prepare to be amazed.

While you are saying the words, imagine yourself feeling happy, or think about a time you remember feeling happy. Perhaps recall a fun vacation or a fond memory of a loved one or pet. Let that feeling of happiness consume you and spread throughout your entire body.

Remember, what you think about does persist. If you tell yourself these exercises are stupid and won't work, chances are they won't. If you believe you can decide to be happy, chances are you will be happier.

Make a conscious effort to start your morning thinking positive, and see how your day unfolds! I encourage you to do this and every challenge with an open mind and heart. You have nothing to lose and so much to gain!

Questions to Consider:

- Where is the first place my thoughts go in the morning?

- On a scale from 1 to 10, how happy am I most days?

- How happy do I want to be?

Week Two:
Go Where You Want to Go

"Congratulations!
Today is your day!
You're off to Great Places!
You're off and away!"
—Dr. Seuss

Go Where You Want to Go

Do you long to plan a vacation and visit the ocean or mountains? Have you been putting off a weekend trip? When was the last time you had a girls' or guys' night out or simply went to the park or movies?

When you get into the boring routine and the crazy hustle and bustle of everyday life, it's easy to forget or not make time to visit the places you want to go and do the things you want to do. With the daily activities of work, school, or raising children, it often feels as if you don't have time for yourself. One way to feel happiness is to go places you want to go and do things you want to do.

This week dedicate time to going to a few places that you have been putting off. Are there restaurants, parks, shows, or museums in your area that you have been talking about visiting for ages but still haven't been? Do you desire a new haircut, massage, or manicure? This week, try to go to at least two or three of those places.

While doing these activities, try to be fully present. Breathe deeply and soak up the atmosphere. Use all your senses to take it all in. Allow yourself to enjoy your time away from your everyday tasks.

When I first started my happiness and self-love journey, this was one practice I made a priority. There were many things on my personal bucket list I was putting off until I had found my perfect partner to share the experience with. I always imagined going on a date to Griffith Park, walking the Venice Canals, and eating at trendy restaurants with my special someone. I stopped waiting to do the things I thought I would love with my partner and began doing them anyway. I soon discovered I'd been missing out by waiting!

Your time here is precious. You don't want to look back on your life and regret all the things you didn't do. There is no reason to wait. Now is the perfect time!

Questions to Consider:

- What local or distant places of interest do I want to visit?

- What activities are on my bucket list, and where can I go to do them?

- What self-care activities have I been putting off?

Week Three:
Be Genuinely Happy for Others

"Happiness is found when you stop comparing yourself to other people."
—Unknown

Be Genuinely Happy for Others

How do you react when you see someone else doing or having the things you want? Are you jealous or envious, or are you genuinely happy for this person?

Envy and jealousy are low-vibrational, fear-based feelings. By the law of attraction, they attract more situations where you will experience those feelings even more. Envy and jealousy push you further away from what you want, not closer to it.

If someone has your dream job, car, house, relationship, or anything else you desire, that does *not* mean that you cannot have the same thing or something better. If anything, it reiterates that it *is* possible, and with the right mindset you can attract it, too! It is an abundant Universe, and there truly is enough for everyone. Fear-based thoughts imply the opposite.

This week use your jealousy as a guide to show you what is possible for you. When you notice feelings of envy or jealousy, pause and notice what you are feeling. When you recognize this behavior, it is easier to change it. Next, wish that person even more success, happiness, or abundance. Affirm, "The only person I compare myself to is my highest self. The success of others brings me joy and shows me what is possible for me."

In the online coaching world, I hear many success stories of men and women that are killing it in the industry, making high-six or seven figures. I notice the days I am feeling fearful is when I experience the most envy or jealousy. In those moments, I always stop, notice, and forgive my fear-based feelings. I remind myself that if they are where I want to be, I can also get there. Next, I wish them even more success and happiness. I instantly feel better because I changed my thoughts of fear into thoughts of love.

Being genuinely happy for others is an abundant feeling and will, by the law of attraction, attract more abundance into your life.

Questions to Consider:

- What feelings and thoughts come up for me when I see other people doing or having what I want?

- Why do I feel inspired by the accomplishments of some people but not others?

- What in my experiences has led me to believe there is not enough for everyone? Am I ready to release this false belief?

Week Four:
Practice Gratitude

"Nothing new can come into your life
unless you are grateful for what you already have."
—Michael Bernard Beckwith

Practice Gratitude

It is easy to get into a mindset of lack and overlook all the amazing and wonderful things in your life. To attract more abundance into your life you must be thankful for what you already have.

Whether you realize it or not, your life has been graced with much. If you woke up with a roof over your head, a bed to sleep on, clean clothes to wear, and fresh water to drink, that is more than millions of people in the world can say.

Every day write down or say out loud at least five things you are grateful for. When you wake up in the morning, be grateful for another day full of potential, a new beginning, and another chance to live the life of your dreams. Throughout the day, affirm, "Today, my heart is beaming with gratitude for every wonderful person in my life and everything I have."

Personally, I prefer to record in my journal what I am grateful for every night before bed. When I reflect on what I am grateful for, it increases my awareness of and ability to appreciate all that I have. I find that when I use my gratitude journal daily, I am more mindful of how I walk through my day. When I notice myself drifting into fear-based feelings of lack, I focus on gratitude. I switch my thoughts and think about what I do have. I instantly feel lighter and more at peace.

Practicing gratitude is an incredible way to put your life into perspective. When you are mindful of what you have, you are more likely to appreciate how much you have. I hope you'll choose to continue to practice gratitude even after completing this weekly challenge—you'll be astounded by the life-changing results!

Questions to Consider:

- What am I grateful for?

- How have the things and people that I view as important in my life changed over time?

- What has consistently been important to me?

- Do I take time to notice all the goodness I already have in my life?

Week Five:
Play Your Happy Song

"Music is a moral law.
It gives soul to the universe, wings to the mind,
flight to the imagination, and charm and gaiety to
life and to everything."
—Plato

Play Your Happy Song

Music can have a powerful effect on your state of mind. Songs can be soothing, empowering, touching, and saddening. You most likely have a song that immediately makes you feel happy, powerful, peaceful, or motivated.

On the first day of the challenge, take note of what songs or genre of music put you into a positive state of mind. These will become your "go-to" happy songs for the week. Perhaps you create your own "happy" play list on a music app such as Spotify.

When you experience any low-vibrational feelings such as anger, sadness, fear, or lack, play your happy song or songs and take note of how your mood instantly changes. Let the music overtake you, and don't resist any feelings or emotions that surface. If you feel inspired to dance or sing along, go for it! You could also start your day by listening to your song while you are getting ready for or going into work.

I have two happy songs. The first is "Happy" by Pharrell Williams. This song always puts me in a good mood and makes me feel happy. The second song is "All of the Above" by Maino featuring T-Pain. This song makes me feel motivated and inspired. It reminds me that I can accomplish anything I put my mind to.

Throughout the week notice your thoughts and be aware of when you are experiencing any low-vibrational feelings. When this occurs, act to shift to a higher vibrational state by playing a song that you associate with happiness, abundance, or motivation.

Questions to Consider:

- What are my "go-to" songs?

- What emotions do I feel when I hear these songs?

- What genre of music makes me want to do a happy dance?

Week Six:
Show Yourself Some Self-Love

"The more you love yourself,
the more you recognize how loved you are."
—Robert Holden

Show Yourself Some Self-Love

Your ability to give love and receive love from others often stems from your ability to love yourself. Whether you are single, in a relationship, or married, practicing self-love is crucial. You do not have to be in a relationship to feel loved. And even if you are in a relationship, self-love is key.

You set the stage for how others treat you. If you treat yourself with respect, others will treat you with respect. They will sense that you do not accept anything less. If you do not respect yourself and treat yourself badly, others will think they can get away with treating you badly.

Every day this week, commit to doing at least one act of self-love and appreciation. Some examples are buying yourself a beautiful rose bouquet, cooking a flavorful meal, taking a bubble bath, savoring a bottle of wine, or taking a scenic walk by yourself.

What nice things do you like your friends, family, and partner to do to show you they love you? This week, try to do some of those things for yourself. Just as you need to prioritize time for acts of love with the other person in a relationship, so you need to do with yourself. Some of my favorite acts of self-love are taking a yoga or meditation class, enjoying a manicure and pedicure, and lounging in a sauna.

The relationship you have with yourself will be the longest and most important relationship you develop in your life. Acts of self-love will help make yours a loving and forgiving relationship instead of one filled with disrespect and self-criticism.

Questions to Consider:

- What are my favorite ways to show self-love?

- What thoughts and feelings come up when I think about loving myself?

- How do the important people in my life view self-love?

Week Seven:
Watch Your Language

*"Talk to yourself like you would
to someone you love."*
—*Brene Brown*

Watch Your Language

Do any of these phrases sound familiar to you? "I don't like how I look today!" "I cannot afford to buy this!" "I don't deserve that!"

What you repeatedly think becomes your beliefs. If you continually tell yourself you are not worthy, don't deserve something, or are not good enough, you will begin to believe it. This fear, self-doubt, and negative criticism keeps you from going after what you want and becoming the person that you know deep down you can be.

This week pay attention to your thoughts and self-talk. There is no judgment here, only observation. How often are you talking down to or belittling yourself? Would you talk to your best friend or mother in the same way? I would think not.

When you notice a limiting belief coming to the surface, stop and acknowledge it. Ask yourself, "Where did this belief come from? Is it really true?" Most likely it is not. It is your ego and old paradigm coming to the surface. Perhaps some time in your life you had someone tell or imply something negative to you or a loved one, and you picked up the thought.

Once you have acknowledged a negative thought, notice it without judgment and immediately turn it into a positive one. Instead of saying, "I can't afford to buy this," affirm "I am wealthy in so many ways." Instead of saying "I don't deserve that," say "I am worthy."

When I first truly paid attention to what I was thinking, I was shocked. I could not believe that I had been talking so hatefully to myself for so long. Even with awareness, negative self-talk still comes up for me. However, I am much better at identifying it and acting to change it. I also have more compassion for myself when I do observe the behavior.

It's time to turn belittling thoughts into empowering ones. Be your own #1 cheerleader!

Questions to Consider:

- How do I talk to myself?

- Would I talk to my best friend or family member in the same way?

- What negative statements can I turn into positive ones?

- What words can I say to myself that I would like to hear from a loved one?

Week Eight:
Find Your Happy Place

"Find your happy place and get lost."
—Unknown

Find Your Happy Place

Do you have triggers? Those people, comments, or situations that set you off and cause you to react quickly?

It could be your boss at work who gets under your skin, a loved one always ready with critical comments, a coworker full of anger and resentment, an enraged stranger on the road, or a customer service representative on the phone giving you attitude. These are just a few of the many examples of people and situations that can test your patience and push your buttons.

This week's challenge is to find your happy place—the place where you feel or imagine feeling absolute bliss, where no person or thing can irritate or annoy you. Maybe your happy place is somewhere you have never been but dream of visiting. For me, that is a beach on a warm, sunny day, or trips as a child camping with my family.

When you find yourself in those moments that test you, or you simply want to feel more peaceful, take a deep breath and imagine yourself in your happy place. This will help shift your mood and give you a chance to stop and think before you react, possibly saying or doing something you later regret.

When you are triggered this week, affirm, "I don't wish to think about this any longer. I choose to think about my happy place and no longer give power to my negative triggers!" Feel the peace wash over your   body and lift your mood.

With practice, it gets easier to imagine yourself in your happy place.

Questions to Consider:

- Who or what are my triggers?

- Where is my happy place?

- How do I feel, or imagine feeling, when I am there?

Week Nine:

Take a Compliment

"I can live for two months on a good compliment."
—Mark Twain

Take a Compliment

How do you react when someone gives you a compliment? Do you blush, look away, mumble a thank-you, or feel the need to compliment the person who complimented you?

Often our human nature leads us to give in return every time we get, so if someone gives us a compliment we feel the need to compliment them back. Or sometimes we downplay the compliment because we feel uncomfortable receiving it, or we don't believe it is true because of our own low level of self-esteem and how we view ourselves. As you increase your own self-love and appreciation, it will become easier to accept compliments from others.

This week's challenge is about learning to feel worthy to receive. How can we receive more love, happiness, success, and abundance if we have a difficult time receiving a small compliment?

I challenge you to own every single compliment with pride. Look the other person in the eye and simply say "Thank you." Relish in the moment.

When I first started noticing my own reactions, I found that I would often downplay my outfits or accessories, saying things like, "Oh, this thing? I got it on sale!" If someone told me I looked pretty or complimented my work, I would try to compliment them back or blush and look away. At first it was hard to own it. With practice, I have gotten much better at receiving compliments and now genuinely enjoy and appreciate them.

This week try to accept all compliments with pride and gratitude! Be proud of who you are and what you contribute to the world.

Questions to Consider:

- How does a person who accepts compliments gracefully behave when complimented?

- How do I react when I receive a compliment?

- How do I want to react?

Week Ten:
Get Comfortable with the Mirror

*"Life always mirrors back to us
the feelings we have inside."*
—Louise Hay

Get Comfortable with the Mirror

Two of my favorite authors and spiritual teachers, Louise Hay and Robert Holden, are big advocates of doing mirror work[4, 5]. What is mirror work, you ask?

It is standing in front of the mirror, looking into your own eyes, and thinking or speaking an affirmation of love. Many different affirmations can be used in this practice, including "I totally and completely love and accept myself," "I love you, (enter your first name)," and "I am lovable."

I challenge you to implement this life-changing practice this week. Many times throughout the day you see your reflection—when getting ready to go out, doing your hair and makeup, checking your appearance, or glancing in the rearview mirror. Take a moment and really look at yourself. Are you rejecting or criticizing yourself?

Notice that it is not the mirror that is judging you. It is your own negative self-talk. The mirror simply reflects what you choose to see. Decide to push any negative thoughts out of your head and instead affirm that you totally and completely love and accept yourself.

What do you notice as you say affirming words in the mirror for the first time? If it feels too much for you, add "I am willing to" before your affirmation. For instance, "I am willing to love and accept myself" and "I am willing to believe I am lovable."

When I first tried doing mirror work I felt all sorts of emotions, from disbelief to sadness and embarrassment. As I continued to do the exercise, I began to feel empowered and started to believe the words I was saying. It is a powerful exercise and one I hope you will do with an open mind.

This week choose to look into the mirror and see all the love and beauty that is you. You so deserve it!

Questions to Consider:

- What feelings or expressions do I see on my face when I look in the mirror?

- How do I feel after saying I love myself?

- Is my reaction to saying affirmations of love changing in any way over time?

Week Eleven:
Love Your Enemies

"Happiness is loving your enemies."
—Charles M. Schulz

Love Your Enemies

Is there someone who currently annoys, irritates, or pisses you off?

Maybe you've had an altercation and are no longer speaking. Or maybe they are clueless and have no idea how you feel. It could be a family member, old friend, coworker, or a goody two-shoes classmate that provokes you.

The challenge of the week is to send them love and positive energy every day. You can do this by thinking a loving thought, saying a prayer or blessing, or imagining having a loving conversation with that person.

Have you ever noticed that no matter how you feel about someone or try to express it, that person often has no idea about your feelings or is not as affected as you would think? Holding grudges, or hanging on to guilt, resentment, and anger hurts only you. Sending love is for you; it's not for that person.

When I first did this exercise, I was holding on to so much anger and sadness. I blamed others for my feelings and didn't want to take responsibility for my part. This exercise changed my life. Each time I did it, I felt lighter. I noticed the pain, tension, and knots in my back begin to disappear. What I was holding onto was not hurting anyone but myself. Love really does heal.

This week as you start and end your day, think of that person and send only love and positivity. Remember, this is healing for *you*. When you send love, especially to someone you feel may not deserve it, you are increasing your vibration. You will allow more love, happiness, success, and abundance to flow your way.

Questions to Consider:

- Who do I currently harbor resentment or anger towards?

- How much energy am I spending holding onto these negative feelings?

- How is this hurting me?

Week Twelve:
Pay It Forward

"To give is to receive—this is the law of Love.
Under this law, when we give our
Love away to others we gain,
and whatever we give we simultaneously receive."
—Gerald Jampolsky

Pay It Forward

It is so important to give to others. There is much truth behind clichés such as "The more you give, the more you receive" and "The more you give, the more you get." Giving to others is rewarding and fulfilling. It puts life into perspective and shows us how fortunate we are.

Every day this week ask yourself, "How can I give today?" Do one random act of kindness without expecting anything in return. There are countless ways to pay it forward. Some examples are to sign up to volunteer for a cause, pick up a stranger's bill, give an unexpected tip, or carry someone's groceries.

I deeply love giving and have since I was a child. I know the power of giving and have witnessed how our selflessness comes back to us in spades. When I am feeling down, one way that always helps me feel better is to give or be of service.

I'll always remember one way that I paid it forward. One year when I was home from California, I helped my mom's church with the giving tree, a program that gives gifts to children in need at the holidays. One woman wanted to give her children a lovely Christmas. She was saddened by her current situation and was noticeably upset on her way to the car. I stopped her in the parking lot and gave her a donation. She started to cry. I started to cry, too, and she hugged me. That moment was so powerful.

She will never know how much I received. The truth is, that week I was questioning becoming a life coach. Fear and self-doubt were getting the best of me. She reminded me how much I love to give and that this career was exactly what I wanted and needed.

Giving with no expectations is an act of love and abundance. By the law of attraction, you will you attract more love and abundance to yourself when you give.

Questions to Consider:

- How do I feel when I give?

- In what ways can I pay it forward?

- Do I have any special skills, talents, or resources to share with others?

- What, besides money, am I willing to give?

Week Thirteen:
Spread the Love

"Love is who you are."
—*Robert Holden*

Spread the Love

If you want to feel love you should first acknowledge that you *are* love. Your soul is the essence of love.

We are all made of love and always have the power to choose love over fear. Remember this as you are practicing this week's challenge. When you give love, you feel love; and when you feel love, you attract love.

The challenge of the week is to spread love to others. Everyday tell at least one loved one how you feel about them.

You can tell your parents and siblings that you love them, praise a fellow coworker for a job well done, let a friend know how much you value your friendship, and share with your significant other what you admire about him or her.

One of my favorite ways to show others how much I love them is to create lists of all the things I appreciate and admire about them. I give this list to them so they know how I really feel. While writing these lists, I feel myself beaming with love and appreciation for them. I have discovered that when you notice and focus on the positives about someone, you will find more of them.

Like attracts like, and love attracts love. To create more love, spread more love. There is always enough love to go around.

Questions to Consider:

- When was the last time I told a certain loved one how glad I am to have them in my life?

- How do I feel when a loved one expresses their love for me?

- What does it feel like to be around someone who is always sending out loving vibes?

Week Fourteen:
Just Say No

"When you say yes to others,
make sure you aren't saying no to yourself."
—Paulo Coelho

Just Say No

Do you find yourself saying yes to things you want to say no to? Have you ever committed to something with dread and then found a last-minute excuse to flake? Do you feel obligated to commit out of guilt, fear, or pressure and then regret it immediately afterwards?

It's okay to say no or that you can't right now, thank you. You can't be everything to everyone. You must honor how you feel.

If you have too much going on or need a night to yourself, honor that. You do not have to commit to every single event, dinner invitation, or family gathering you are invited to. This can lead to your feeling resentful, worn out, and drained. It is important to establish open communication in these situations and to be honest about your own needs.

The important lesson behind this week's challenge is honoring yourself and establishing boundaries. This week when someone asks you to do something that you don't want to do, politely say no or ask to reschedule for another time. It's better to decline than to cancel later or do something that does not serve you at that moment.

Saying no can feel uncomfortable at first, just as it was for me. I said yes when I shouldn't have and ended up cancelling plans more often that I'd like to admit. When I started putting boundaries into place and respecting my time and feelings, I felt more like myself. And now when I do make plans, I truly enjoy them.

Even if it is not in your nature, it is okay to say no. Your friends, family, and loved ones will all benefit from you being true to yourself.

Questions to Consider:

- What current situations in my life have I committed to out of guilt or pressure?

- How could I have politely declined?

- What will I do this week if that opportunity comes up again?

Week Fifteen:
Make Complaining a Thing of the Past

"Complaining is finding faults;
wisdom is finding solutions."
—Ajahn Brahm

Make Complaining a Thing of the Past

How many times a day do you catch yourself complaining about something? "I am tired." "My boss is a jerk!" "My spouse is getting on my nerves!" "I can't afford anything!" "Traffic was horrible!" It's possible you might even be doing it without realizing it.

When you complain, you focus on the negatives in your life. The things you continue to think and talk about will come about through the law of attraction. If you want a different experience, it is important not to give attention and energy to what you do not want or like. If you do, this results in your manifesting more of what you don't want. Instead, focus on the positives, or what you do want.

This week when you feel yourself starting to complain about something, pause. Try to see the positives in the situation or decide to think about something else. Another option is to try to think of a solution to the problem you are facing. If you feel frustrated, let it out in another way, such as going for a walk, working out, or hitting or yelling into a pillow.

I know I never feel good when I complain. It makes me feel worse or the same, but never better. What does help me is thinking of creative solutions to whatever problem or struggle I'm facing. So, try to channel your frustrations into creative solutions instead of unproductive complaints.

Taking action almost always feels better than standing by and complaining—and you just may end up solving a problem, too.

Questions to Consider:

- What do I frequently vent or complain about?

- How can I turn my complaints into creative solutions?

- How do I decide when I should try to change things or when I should try to accept them?

Week Sixteen:
Laugh Out Loud

"A day without laughter is a day wasted."
—Charlie Chaplin

Laugh Out Loud

You have likely heard the saying "Laughter is the best medicine." As it turns out, laughing *is* good for you! It does wonders for both your body and soul.

Based on results of numerous studies on human behavior and physiology, happiness expert and meditation instructor Tamara Lechner summarizes that the positive side effects of laughter include less stress, boosted immunity, increased resilience, pain relief, and reduced depression.[6]

Imagine how great your life would be with less stress, pain, and depression; a stronger immune system; and more resilience and happiness! Sounds amazing!

The challenge of the week is to do activities that make you laugh and to spend time laughing every day. Perhaps you go see a comedy show, put on your favorite rom com, have a tickle fight, watch funny videos online, or reminisce with friends, all for the sake of enjoying a great laugh.

When I am feeling down and in need of a pick-me-up, I love to watch stand-up comedy. My mood instantly lifts! I love how comedians can find humor in almost every situation and human emotion and make it so comically relatable.

So, lift your mood and get yourself feeling great this week with plenty of LOL (laughing out loud).

Questions to Consider:

- What makes me laugh out loud?

- How can I add more laughter and lightheartedness into my life this week?

- Do I have a person in my life that always makes me laugh?

Week Seventeen:
Focus on an Abundance of Time

"Time is an illusion."
—Albert Einstein

Focus on an Abundance of Time

Do you ever struggle with time management? Do you feel that there is not enough time in your day to get everything done? Are you always running late?

As you are aware, what you think becomes your reality. If you believe you never have enough time to get everything done, you won't get everything done. If you always focus on being late, you will be late.

The challenge this week is to become aware of your thoughts and words about time. At the start of each day, affirm, "I always have plenty of time to get things done." As you notice yourself being stressed or worried about not being able to finish your to-do list, take a deep breath and repeat the affirmation. If you notice yourself feeling anxious about being on time, pause and affirm, "I am always on time."

I used to run late to most meetings and appointments no matter how early I woke up or how much time I gave myself to get there. When I started thinking and believing I always had enough time and was always on time, I found myself becoming more productive and punctual. Go figure.

Remember, your thoughts become your reality. Don't focus on a lack of time—focus on an abundance of time!

Questions to Consider:

- What are my current thoughts about time?

- Do I feel a lack of time or an abundance of time?

- Do you ever run ahead of time then do something to sabotage yourself?

Week Eighteen:
Be Present

"My preoccupation with the past and its projection into the future defeats any aims of present peace. The past is over and the future is yet to be. Peace cannot be found in the past or future, but only in this instant."
—Gerald Jampolsky

Be Present

Do you tend to live in the past and constantly want to re-create it? Are you preoccupied with what may happen in the future? Neither of these situations are ideal because both cause you to lose focus on the present.

When you are always looking back into the past or anticipating the future, you are not fully living. Things will never be exactly as they were. And what you want for the future may never happen. It is difficult to open to true happiness when you are not living for today.

This week take time to be present. Notice and appreciate things big and little. Use all your senses and skills of observation. Embrace all your emotions. Take note of how wonderful your meal tastes, how funny your significant other is, how pleasant the sun feels on your skin, and how much fun you have on your girls' night out.

As someone who spent much of her life holding on to the past and worrying unnecessarily about the future, I understand now that I welcome the greatest level of happiness in the present.

When you find yourself reminiscing excessively about the past or worrying about the future, take a deep breath, find your center, and remind yourself to be present.

The affirmation for the week is "I always live in the present moment. That is where true happiness lies."

Questions to Consider:

- Do I often find myself looking to the past or future for joy?

- How has this negatively impacted my present level of happiness?

- Why do I think *being present* is often called *being mindful*?

Week Nineteen:
Compliment Yourself

"Say nice things to yourself.
You're the only one listening."
—Gabrielle Bernstein

Compliment Yourself

As noted in the previous challenge Take a Compliment, it's important to accept compliments from others because it gives you a chance to receive with gratitude. Now, ask yourself, "How often do I compliment myself?" Your response may likely be that you hardly ever do. Well, this week that changes!

This week give yourself at least five compliments a day or write down at least five things you love about yourself each day. If you choose to give yourself compliments, do so in front of the mirror.

Compliment yourself as if you were giving a compliment to your best friend, parent, or child—with kindness. If you are doing this exercise as a writing assignment, write at the top of your journal page "5 Things I Love About Me," and list them. You do not have to stop at five. If you're on a roll, keep going!

For me, some of the qualities and characteristics I love and appreciate about myself are my ability to give, my determination and strength, my capacity to love, and my faith and trust in the Universe. I will often write down or say compliments to myself when I notice myself being very critical or engaging in negative self-talk. It instantly brings me out of fear and back to love.

This exercise is important because it gives you the opportunity to both give and receive. It is a great way to express self-love, build self-confidence, and value your abilities. The more you love yourself and appreciate who you are, the happier you will be.

Questions to Consider:

- How often do I compliment myself?

- What positive characteristics or gifts do I have that few people know about?

- What do I love about me?

Week Twenty:
Practice Forgiveness

"The weak can never forgive.
Forgiveness is an attribute of the strong."
—Mahatma Gandhi

Practice Forgiveness

Practicing forgiveness can be a very difficult thing to do. You may be holding on to anger, resentment, jealousy, and other fear-based vibrations. Choosing to not forgive allows those negative vibrations to harm you, holds you in the past, and prevents you from fully living in the present.

Forgiveness is ultimately about you and shows your inner strength. It promotes healing and allows for a deeper level of happiness. Forgiveness does not mean that you condone the actions of the other party involved. It means that you choose to not hold on to the feelings that no longer serve you and that keep you from moving forward. Forgiveness brings peace.

This week, you will be implementing an exercise called the Forgiveness Scale, taught by best-selling Hay House author and founder of the Happiness Project, Robert Holden.[7]

First, think of someone you have less than ideal feelings for, someone you have not completely forgiven in some capacity. If you have not forgiven yourself for something in your past, this person can even be you.

Focus on this person clearly in your mind. On a scale of 0% to 100% how much have you forgiven that person? Reflect on that percentage and write it down. Now ask yourself how this has affected your life and your current level of happiness. Next, increase that number a few percentage points toward 100%. Affirm, "I am willing to forgive (insert person's name) (insert %)." How did that feel? Say it a few times with conviction. Pay attention to what comes up for you.

As you feel less resistance, increase that number a few percentage points and repeat the affirmation. Do this exercise every day for a week and note your progress by checking in with where you are on the forgiveness scale.

If you experience a lot of emotion, journal it out and do not judge what comes up for you. Be gentle and patient with yourself. Forgiveness is a healing and growing process that takes time.

Throughout my life, I held on to so much anger and resentment about my early childhood. It took a long time to realize that I was bringing these fear-based vibrations into my relationships. Forgiving the parties involved helped me create a deeper level of peace and happiness. It finally allowed me to leave the past in the past so I could focus on the present.

Forgiveness is one of the best gifts you can give yourself. You deserve peace, and you can have peace. This challenge helps you get one step closer to it.

Questions to Consider:

- Is there someone that has hurt me?

- Where am I currently on the forgiveness scale?

- How many increases in % forgiveness do I think it will take before I feel a difference in my peace and happiness levels?

- Am I ready to forgive 100%?

Week Twenty-One:
Protect Your Energy

*"Stop giving your precious energy
to things that make you feel bad."*
—Louise Hay

Protect Your Energy

Do you ever feel drained around certain people or situations and you don't know why? Do you often feel a little "off" after being in a large room full of people?

You were likely picking up on someone else's negative or low-vibration energy.

This week, to keep your energy as positive and high-vibe as possible, try adopting one or more energy-protecting practices. You can focus on protecting your energy in several ways, so be sure to explore and find the one or two that work best for you.

Each morning you can meditate and visualize yourself surrounded by a white healing light or a bubble of protection. This light or bubble shields you and allows only high-vibrational energy to flow through to you. During this practice, if the power of angels resonates with you, call on Archangel Michael to protect and shield your energy and aura. (Michael is the archangel of protection and will help keep you safe from any fear-based or negative energies.)

Or try a different method. Throughout the day, as you hear or see someone being negative, imagine yourself sweeping those negative words or actions away from you. You can also use your hand to do a sweeping motion, acknowledging to yourself that you do not wish to take that negativity on as your own.

A few other common practices for energy protection are holding, wearing, or carrying crystals known for absorbing and transmuting negative energy, such as black tourmaline, black onyx, and smoky quartz; burning or smudging sage; spending time outside in nature to help keep your energy pure; and affirming, "I am safe and protected. My energy is only of the highest vibration and my thoughts are positive. I choose to surround myself with truly loving people and circumstances."

I spent most my life unaware that certain people and situations drained my energy. I would often feel heavy or weird after being around negative people or large crowds. I did not realize I was picking up some of that energy and taking it on as my own. It was exhausting. I would feel tired and in desperate need of time alone. Once I learned some of these practices to protect my energy, I felt better mentally and physically, as I hope you will too.

Your energy is precious, and it is important to know how to protect it properly.

Questions to Consider:

- What will I do this week to protect my precious energy?

- Am I an empath, or a highly sensitive person that takes on other people's emotions?

- Do I make it a priority to be alone specifically to recharge my energy?

Week Twenty-Two:
Clear Your Energy

"Smile with face, smile with mind,
and good energy will come to you and
clean away dirty energy."
—Elizabeth Gilbert

Clear Your Energy

Last week's challenge was Protect Your Energy. Now that you feel more confident about how to protect your energy, this week you will learn how to clear it. It is important to clear your energy when you feel as if you have picked up someone else's negative emotions or you yourself are feeling negative. Just as with protecting your energy, there are several ways to clear your energy, so be sure to try a couple of methods to find the ones that suit you best.

Before bed, meditate and visualize the cords being cut that connect you to the people and situations that affected you negatively during the day. If you are a coach, healer, or teacher, it is also important to do this exercise after each client interaction, so that you do not absorb your client's energy. While doing this exercise, you can call on Archangel Michael, if he resonates with you, to cut the cords with his powerful sword. (He is the archangel of protection and will help cut any cords of negativity or attachment.)

You can also sweep or move your hand out in front of your body, from left to right. This motion acknowledges that you are clearing your energy. If it does not feel clear after one time, continue the motion until it does. You can also move your hand out in front of your body from the top of your head to your toes, pushing any negative energy into the earth to be transmuted. Again, repeat until your energy feels clearer.

Other great practices include listening to an energy-clearing or chakra-clearing guided meditation; burning sage or smudging your house, belongings, or surroundings; taking a salt bath or scrubbing your body with salt, imagining all the negativity going down the drain with the water; using essential oils that help clear any negative energy around you, such as rose, lavender, frankincense, and sage; going barefoot in nature and grounding yourself into the earth; and affirming, "I am free and clear. My energy is only of the highest vibration and my thoughts are positive."

Your energy is sacred and it is important to know how to clear it properly. When I practice these clearing exercises, I instantly feel lighter and brighter. I wish the same for you.

Questions to Consider:

- How can I tell when my energy has been affected?

- Are there certain people that easily affect my energy?

- What will I do to clear my energy this week?

Week Twenty-Three:
Create an Empowering Morning Ritual

*"A daily ritual is a way of saying,
'I'm voting for myself;
I'm taking care of myself.'"*
—Mariel Hemingway

Create an Empowering Morning Ritual

What do some of the most successful and inspiring spiritual and business leaders have in common?

They all have daily morning rituals. What those rituals entail depends on the person, but they each start their day with practices that encourage self-love and improvement.

It is important to start and end each day feeling good. If you go to bed angry, sad, or stressed out, chances are you will wake up in the morning feeling the same way. However, if you make the decision to start your day feeling good and create a practice that encourages positivity, chances are you will continue to feel good throughout the day.

This week's challenge is for you to create a daily morning ritual. Your ritual should feel authentic to you and help set the tone for the rest of your day.

Some examples of practices you can incorporate into your morning ritual include meditating and praying, saying aloud or writing affirmations and mantras, visualizing, working out or stretching, practicing gratitude, doing mirror work (saying loving affirmations in front of a mirror), drinking a warm soothing beverage such as herbal tea, and journaling.

My morning ritual includes reading affirmations, visualizing the life I want to create, meditating, and reading self-help and wealth-consciousness books. I also read daily from the metaphysical text *A Course in Miracles*. I can honestly say I notice a huge difference in myself and my ability to manage my emotions on the days that I do my morning ritual. It truly makes my day more positive and empowering because feeling good in the morning leads to feeling good throughout the day.

Questions to Consider:

- Do I currently have a morning ritual?

- If so, do I do it daily?

- What practices do I want to include in my morning ritual to start my day feeling good?

- How am I affected when I pick up an electronic device, such as a smartphone or tablet, or turn on the television before I begin my morning ritual?

Week Twenty-Four:
Set Boundaries

*"Boundaries are a part of self-care.
They are healthy, normal, and necessary."*
—*Doreen Virtue*

Set Boundaries

Are there relationships in your life in which you feel as if you are being taken advantage of in some way? Is someone doing something hurtful or that makes you feel resentful? If so, does this person know how you feel? Have you set and established boundaries with this person?

Boundaries are vital in any type of relationship. It is important to know what your limits are and clearly communicate them to avoid future conflict.

Does your partner know it bothers you when he or she talks about past relationships? Does your boss know not to call you when you are taking time off? Do your children know how they are expected to help around the house? Do vendors and potential clients know that you do not barter in your business?

These situations are examples of when boundaries could be implemented. If you do not set and assertively communicate boundaries, you cannot expect others to honor and respect them.

This week determine, set, and implement boundaries. First, determine where in your life you need to set boundaries and what these boundaries should be. Next, communicate those boundaries in the most loving and assertive way possible. The boundaries will be ineffective if no one knows that you have set them. Once those boundaries are set and communicated, implement them.

Don't be afraid to speak up in a clear but direct way when someone pushes or crosses boundaries. Depending on the person and circumstance, you may need to write out or establish guidelines, policies, or procedures to better help implement your boundaries.

When I first started my coaching business, I hadn't set clear boundaries. I would get messages from people wanting free advice and coaching. A few clients would try to reschedule our coaching calls at the last minute or not submit payment in a timely manner. When I set boundaries on how and when members could contact me and implemented a stricter nonrefundable cancellation and payment policy, people respected them. These issues were no longer issues. I now have these policies in my client contract and will reference them if any questions or special requests arise.

Communication is key here. Setting boundaries sets the tone for how others treat you, whatever the type of relationship. Stand by the boundaries you implement and do not be surprised if the Universe tests you to see if you are serious!

Questions to Consider:

- In what areas of my life do I need to set boundaries?

- What should these boundaries look like?

- What is the best way to implement and enforce these boundaries?

Week Twenty-Five:
Listen to Your Intuition

"Intuition is seeing with the soul."
—Dean Koontz

Listen to Your Intuition

Have you ever had a strong feeling that you should or should not do something, and you didn't know why? Have you ever had a gut feeling about someone with no real explanation as to why you felt that way? Your intuition and your inner guidance system were guiding you during these times.

Your predominant thoughts are heavily influenced by your ego. Your ego works to keep you as safe from failure as possible through what sounds like logic but that is often based in fear. Fear is the ego's way of protecting you. When you're making a decision, your ego is the part of your mind that tells you you're not good enough, smart enough, or deserving enough. The ego is an illusion of who you think you are.

Your intuition is the piece of your soul that wants you to be who you really are—your higher, authentic self. It always guides you to make the right decisions.

This week, when you are faced with a decision and need guidance, I challenge you to call on your intuition. Step away from your current situation and take a deep breath. Close your eyes and focus on your breath. Ask your intuition, "What do I need to know? What is the best decision for me?" Then listen and allow yourself to receive any messages that come through. They may sound like your own thinking voice or someone else's completely. If you find this exercise difficult, you can try free writing. Call on your intuition for guidance as just described, but then write whatever comes up for you. Do not filter as you write.

Since learning more about how to tap into my intuition, I now rely on it to make all the major decisions in my life. In fact, I followed my intuition about leaving my full-time job and becoming a life coach and author.

Your intuition is a part of you that wants you to be truly happy. Make a change if need be, and follow your heart. It will guide you to where you're meant to be.

Questions to Consider:

- How does my intuition communicate to me?

- In times when I did not listen to my intuition, what was the outcome?

- What will I do to connect with my intuition?

Week Twenty-Six:
Identify What Brings You Joy

"Enjoy being with yourself,
hanging out with yourself,
doing things by yourself."
—Frederick Lenz

Identify What Brings You Joy

Have you ever sat down and identified what activities bring you joy? What lights you up, makes you smile, or brings you peace? What are your favorite pastimes and hobbies?

The challenge this week is to write down everything and anything you can think of that you enjoy doing. You can write these down in your journal, or type them on your computer or phone.

The act of creating the detailed list of your favorite joyful activities is a great way to focus on self-care and self-love and is a time- and energy-saving activity. It is important to keep this list readily available so that you can refer to it often and not have to think of things to do that will make you feel better when you are feeling down.

This week commit to doing at least one thing from this list every day. The more you focus on doing the activities that bring you joy, the more joy you will experience.

My life coach encouraged me to create this list two years ago. I keep my list in my journal and refer to it often and make updates as needed. When I am having a bad day, I make it a priority to do something from the list to help change my mood and shift my vibration. Some activities on my list include taking a yoga class, meditating, hiking, going to the park, spending time at the beach, and visiting gardens.

Even though we know what brings us joy, sometimes we may still need a push to do them. We're so glad afterward, but sometimes it takes some effort to get started. I never regret taking the time to do the things I love, and I know you won't either. Now it is your time to make doing joy-filled activities a priority.

Questions to Consider:

- What activities that bring me joy will I list?

- How often do I do these activities?

- How does it feel to commit to choosing my bliss every day?

Week Twenty-Seven:
Put a Smile on Your Face

"Keep smiling,
because life is a beautiful thing
and there's so much to smile about."
—Marilyn Monroe

Put a Smile on Your Face

Did you know your mood can change based on your facial expression?

Brain and behavior expert Roger Dooley noted, "Your mood is elevated and your stress is reduced if you plaster a big smile on your face, even for a short period of time."[8] The same holds true if you fake a smile but do not truly feel the emotion. Studies show that frowning can have the opposite effect. Simply put, if you want to change how you feel, change your facial expression!

You have likely noticed that being around people who are smiling makes you want to smile. Smiling is contagious and makes others around you feel good.

This week, smile...as often as possible. Pay attention to your facial expression throughout the day. Are you catching yourself frowning or scowling? If so, then smile, even if it's forced. Set reminders on your phone, post smiley-face sticky notes around your house and office, and even tell your friends and family to remind you to smile.

This is one of my favorite challenges and is very simple—and free! It is one of the first exercises my life coach had me focus on. Smiling makes me feel joyful. Anytime I smile, I instantly feel a warmth coming from the center of my chest, my mood quickly shifts, and I immediately feel less stressed.

Remember that your radiant smile can help change your day as well as those around you.

Questions to Consider:

- How often do I smile throughout the day?

- How does my mood change once I smile, even if it is forced?

- What thoughts or memories always bring a smile to my face?

Week Twenty-Eight:
Spend Time Outside

*"In every walk with nature
one receives far more than he seeks."*
—John Muir

Spend Time Outside

Where do you feel the most at peace? Is it at your favorite park? In a garden? At the beach?

Chances are it's somewhere outside, in nature. It is likely that your mood shifts when you step outside, and there is a reason why. According to research examined by health writer and editor Abigail Wise, being outside reduces stress levels and puts you in a positive mood. It also increases creativity and brain function.[9]

This week strive to spend at least 10 minutes outside every single day and simply be present. Breathe deeply and use as many senses as possible. Allow yourself to take in the sights, smells, and sounds. Be observant of the temperature and movement of the air around you. Instead of going to the gym, run or walk outside. Instead of eating at your desk or in your cubicle, eat lunch outside. Instead of reading in the house, sit on the porch.

I know, for me, being outside even for a short period shifts my mood drastically. It is also where I feel the most connected to God and my intuition. When my fiancé notices that I am feeling sad or not like myself, he often encourages me to spend time outside. He can see firsthand what a positive effect it has on me. I usually come back in as a more upbeat and loving version of myself.

Take advantage of the beautiful nature around you and give your soul the fresh air and sunshine it is craving.

Questions to Consider:

- What is my favorite outdoor spot?

- What outside activities am I going to do this week?

- Do the sounds of nature—birds singing and frogs croaking—lift my spirit?

Week Twenty-Nine:
Give Positive Words of Affirmation

*"One kind word can change
someone's entire day."*
—Unknown

Give Positive Words of Affirmation

Do you let other people know how amazing they are? Do you commend others for a job well done? Do you try to lift someone up when they are having a bad day?

Think about how you feel when someone tells you you're extraordinary, recognizes your dedication and hard work, or reminds you that everything is going to be okay. Incredible, I bet. That's because hearing positive words of affirmation can lift your mood and have a tremendous impact on your day.

Every day this week, give positive words of affirmation to at least one person you see. You can tell your father he is remarkable, remind a friend who is struggling that she is powerful and capable of anything, or let a coworker know that you appreciate his or her important contribution to a project. Make sure that your words of affirmation are said intentionally with no distractions, and that the other person clearly hears your words. Really make this moment of kindness count!

Often, giving other people positive words of affirmation can feel even better than receiving them. When I go out of my way to say considerate things to others, I walk away with a warmth in my heart and a new energy in my step.

Do not underestimate the power of positivity. A few simple words of kindness can make a huge impact.

Questions to Consider:

- How often do I give positive words of affirmation to others?

- Is there someone who I recognize as different in some way—someone who is always kind to others, someone whose life is full of challenges, or something else like this.

- Who will I touch with my words this week?

Week Thirty:
Cheer Someone Up

"The best way to cheer yourself up is to cheer somebody else up."
—Mark Twain

Cheer Someone Up

Have you been in a funk lately? Are you trying to shift to a more positive mindset, but you don't know how?

When you help someone, you take your attention off your own current problem or situation and focus on someone else's. Doing something to better another person's life can help change your perspective and bring about a deep and rewarding sense of inner peace.

This week focus on being of service by cheering someone up. If you are feeling down, focus your attention on someone else. Reach out to a friend, family member, or coworker who needs some extra love and support. Call, send a text, give a hug, or simply offer an ear to listen. Another option is to send flowers or a small gift.

Try to keep any conversation positive and offer potential solutions to address the problem. Focus on empathizing with the person, but do not commiserate with them. Letting the conversation spiral into negativity will not serve either of you.

Many times over the past year I focused on being of service when I was feeling down. In these moments, I often do a Facebook live stream where I allow my community to ask me questions, and I coach them on those topics. During these conversations, I try to listen, suggest action items, and direct the conversation back to the positive when needed. After the live streams, my mood always lifts, and I feel a sense of peace and happiness within myself. It feels fantastic to be able to help others in such a positive way.

When you shift your mindset from being sad or upset to being of service, you lift yourself up and bring positivity and love to someone else. This will raise both your own vibration and the vibration of that person. Plus, it will strengthen the bond of the relationship between the two of you.

Questions to Consider:

- Have I ever talked to someone about my problems and felt worse afterward?

- Do I think the saying "Misery loves company" is true?

- Who in my life has been having a hard time?

- How can I help boost his or her mood this week?

Week Thirty-One:
Awaken Your Inner Child

"The secret of genius is to carry the spirit of the child into old age, which means never losing your enthusiasm."
—Aldous Huxley

Awaken Your Inner Child

Think about your childhood. What were some fun things you did during that time? What activities absolutely lit you up and brought you joy? Some of my favorite pastimes were swinging, riding roller coasters, playing at the water park, and spending the day at the beach with my older sister, Sarah.

If your energy has been feeling a little stagnant lately, it might be that your soul is craving playtime! Now is the time to give yourself what you need.

This week is all about awakening your inner child through play. For some, it might mean doing some of those favorite childhood activities. For others, it might mean spending time playing with your own children or adding more play into your normal routine.

This week ask yourself, "What does my inner child want to do today?" and "What activities feel like play for me?" Perhaps you buy an adult—or a kid's—coloring book, ride your bike, or play your favorite childhood movie. Maybe you go to an amusement park, attend a ball game, join a sports league, or take a dance class.

This week is also the perfect time to make mundane daily activities more fun. For instance, play your favorite songs or listen to a podcast during your commute, sing and dance while doing the dishes, or watch your favorite program while folding the laundry.

Whatever you choose to do this week, make sure it feels like play.

Questions to Consider:

- What childhood activities would I love to do this week?

- How can I add more play to my normal routine?

- What silly songs, games, or riddles from my childhood do I share with the kids in my life?

Week Thirty-Two:
Talk Kindly About Others

"Strong people do not put others down...
They lift them up."
—Michael P. Watson

Talk Kindly About Others

Every workplace, school, friend group, and family has its gossipers. This is something you cannot control. What you can control is if you choose to partake in the gossip.

This week notice how you react when someone talks negatively about someone else. There is no self-judgment here; you are simply observing your patterns. Do you engage in the gossip? Do you change the subject and walk away, or simply refuse to partake? Or do you try to counteract the negative by saying something kind about the person the gossiper is talking about?

This week's challenge is to show compassion in your words about others. You never truly know what someone else is going through, or why they act the way they do. In fact, you may not know that the gossip being said about that person is true at all. If you were the subject of the gossip of the day, would you want others to speak badly about you? Of course not.

This challenge is one that I continuously work to improve upon. Without being deliberately mindful of what I and others are saying, it can be easy to get caught up in gossip and not even realize it, and I have found this to be very true for myself. Once I started tuning in, I noticed that gossip was all around me, and I was often right in the middle of it.

As soon as I notice myself being judgmental or mean-spirited, or as soon as I leave these negative conversations, I instantly regret my behavior. Talking meanly about others never makes me feel good. I think that often the reason I do it is that something unhealed that I recognize in the person also lies within my own shadow.

With practice, this challenge does get easier. Have kind words for others even when you're speaking about them and not to them. You can be the example. You can show kindness and love, even behind a person's back.

Questions to Consider:

- When and how often do I gossip about others?

- Are there particular people or topics that draw me into participating in negative conversations?

- How do I feel when I gossip about others?

- What words or actions can I have ready to stop me from engaging in gossip?

Week Thirty-Three:
Give Yourself Permission to Unplug

"Almost everything will work again if you unplug it for a few minutes, including you."
—Anne Lamott

Give Yourself Permission to Unplug

We live in a fast-paced society filled with to-do lists and multitasking. Being on the go is the new norm, and we are always connected to our phones, computers, and tablets. This hectic lifestyle can be draining, leaving us feeling depleted from always being "on."

This challenge is about taking time off when you need to and giving yourself permission to unplug. When you have a daunting to-do list this may be easier said than done. This week try to unplug as much as possible, and schedule some time for yourself. Perhaps you take a day off from work, hire a babysitter, or simply turn off your phone for a few hours.

As someone who works closely with the emotions and well-being of others, I grow exhausted when I do not give myself time to unplug. I often go to my room for some alone time to rest and restore my energy at the end of the night. I remove myself from my phone to allow myself the space that I need. When I don't give myself time to unplug, not only do I suffer, but the people close to me suffer. I become very irritable at these times and am not nice to be around.

Remember that unplugging is nonnegotiable. The to-do list can wait. Your health and well-being cannot. When you allow yourself to have the time and space you need to care for yourself, you will be more likely to return to your normal activities refreshed and more productive.

Questions to Consider:

- When was the last time I gave myself the chance to unplug?

- How many electronic devices am I connected to at any given moment?

- How am I going to unplug this week?

Week Thirty-Four:
Reflecting on Gratitude

*"Gratitude to God is to accept everything,
even my problems, with joy."*
—Mother Teresa

Reflecting on Gratitude

During the earlier challenge Practice Gratitude you were asked to identify what you were grateful for. This week you will further expand upon that idea, as you will not only identify what you are grateful for but also why you are grateful for it.

Every day this week, write down at least five people, places, or things you are grateful for, and why. This exercise is an excellent way to look back over your life and reflect about who you are today.

What things and places are you grateful for, and what do they mean to you? What people and situations entered into your life, and what did they teach you? Did they make you stronger, teach you an important lesson, or help mold you into the person you are today? Why are you thankful for them?

As I mentioned earlier, I dated a lot of guys who were not looking for a serious relationship. At the time, it was very painful for me. Now, looking back on that time in my life, I am so grateful for it. Also hurtful was my being passed up for several promotions at work. At the time, I was angry and resentful. Now, I am grateful.

You see, both situations contributed to the reason I began my own self-love and happiness journey. If my love life had been satisfying and my work life had been fulfilling, I may not have developed the desire to focus on myself and make positive changes. For that, I am so grateful because the person I have become is someone I am proud to be. I would not have been able to say that with the same confidence even a few years ago.

This exercise helps you identify ways in which you are already abundant. Here, you are not only reflecting on what you have, but you are remembering why what you have is important to you.

Questions to Consider:

- What am I grateful for this week, and why?

- Are there particular situations in my life that have been especially difficult or rewarding?

- What does being grateful for certain things help me understand about who I am?

Week Thirty-Five:
Cry If You Want To

"Cry. Forgive. Learn. Move on.
Let your tears water the seeds
of your future happiness."
—Steve Maraboli

Cry If You Want To

We live in a society that often tells us to suppress our emotions. Phrases such as "Big girls don't cry" and "cry baby" give negative connotation to crying. As a result, many people see crying as showing weakness. They are not aware that the act of crying is good for you!

According to *WebMD* magazine's Serusha Govender, crying leads to many health benefits, such as reduction of stress, release of muscle tension, and activation of the parasympathetic nervous system, which helps keep balance in the body.[10] For instance, when I cry, I instantly feel lighter. That deep sense of release is often exactly what I need.

This week try not to hold back your emotions. If you feel the need to cry, go for it, without guilt or shame. Afterward, affirm, "It is safe for me to cry and express all my emotions. I love and accept myself fully."

I am a deeply emotional person, and it doesn't take much to start me crying. I'm okay with that. In fact, I am proud of allowing myself to embrace all my emotions. Crying is okay, and I accept that.

This week's challenge is not just about crying or expressing your emotions. It's also about loving yourself through the process. You are lovable no matter what you are feeling.

Questions to Consider:

- Do I believe it is safe to cry?

- Do I often hold back my tears or other emotions?

- Do I find it easier to smile or laugh than to cry?

- What other ways do I express emotions besides crying?

Week Thirty-Six:
Releasing Fear

"Everything you want
is on the other side of fear."
—Jack Canfield

Releasing Fear

Fear is real and can often be very intense.

This week's exercise is about getting real with your fears and releasing them with love. With practice, you can become aware of the fearful thoughts that prevent you from living fully and begin to choose new thought patterns.

Every night before bed, make a list of all the fears that came up for you throughout the day. Perhaps you noticed yourself judging others, had feelings of lack, or were afraid to doing something you wanted to do. Write down these fears on a piece of paper or in your journal.

After you have made your list, reread your fears one by one. After each, affirm, "I forgive and release this fear with love." Imagine the fear leaving your mind and spirit and dissolving into the air, transmuting into positive, loving energy. For further support, call on God and your angels to help you during this practice.

After the affirmations, sit for a few minutes in silence, lovingly reflecting on and acknowledging any feelings that surface. If you would like, you can tear up or burn your list of fears after you have completed the exercise.

I find releasing my fears to be both cleansing and empowering, which makes room for more peace and happiness. I make an effort to do this every month or as often as needed.

If you find that you are having a difficult time with the affirmations and are limited for now to merely being willing to release your fears with love, know that achieving even this level will still make a remarkable shift in your life.

Questions to Consider:

- What fears continuously come up for me?

- Which fears do I find limit me most?

- Do I find it is difficult to release some fears more than others?

- How do I feel once I lovingly release these fears?

Week Thirty-Seven:
Say I Love You

"The best way to be loved
is to love yourself."
—Adam Lambert

Say I Love You

How often do you tell the people in your life—family, friends, and your significant other, if you have one—that you love them?

Now, how often do you tell yourself that you love you? I would guess not as often, if at all. This week's challenge will help change that.

Every night before bed and every morning upon waking, place both hands over your heart and affirm, "I love you, (insert your name)." If this is too much for you, you can add the word *willing* to the affirmation: "I am willing to love you, (insert your name)." Don't move on too quickly. Remain in the moment, feeling and appreciating the magnitude of your words. Imagine a loving pink light emerging from your chest and wrapping you in warm, healing energy.

Before my own self-love journey, I cannot easily recall a time when I told myself that I loved me. Now, I try to make it a daily habit. Besides, do you ever get sick of being told that someone loves you? It really does not matter who that someone is: love is love. But it is especially important that those words come from you.

This challenge addresses cultivating and nurturing the most important relationship of all—the one you have with yourself! Having a strong sense of self-love is the foundation for living a happy, successful, abundant, and fulfilling life. Self-love is the keystone for all the other relationships in your life, so take the time to remind yourself that you love you, or that you are willing to love you!

Questions to Consider:

- What comes up for me when I say "I love you" to myself?

- Am I comfortable with myself or do I feel awkward?

- Do I feel fear or other emotions based in fear?

Week Thirty-Eight:
Thank and Praise Your Body

"Take care of your body.
It's the only place you have to live."
—Jim Rohn

Thank and Praise Your Body

Think about how much time you spend criticizing your body, projecting thoughts like, "I hate my wrinkles," "I have cellulite," and "I look gross right now."

Now, think about how much time you spend thanking and praising your body. I know I would often find myself criticizing my body much more often than praising it.

Remember this: During every single minute of the day, your body is functioning to keep you alive and healthy!

How wonderful is that!?!

Your body pumps blood through your veins and pushes air through your lungs. It allows you to savor your favorite meals and knock out your favorite workouts. Although your body is responsible for everything you do in the physical world, this reality is often overlooked because we focus on the judgments and criticisms instead.

The challenge of the week is to show gratitude for how extraordinary your body is instead of pointing out its faults. Every time you notice yourself criticizing a part of your body, stop and affirm, "I love and appreciate my body. Thank you for all that you do for me."

What your body does for you every day is truly amazing. It is worthy of praise and gratitude.

Questions to Consider:

- What are my dominant thoughts about my body?

- When was the last time I stopped to thank and praise my body?

- Do I thank my body by allowing it nourishment and rest when it has worked hard?

Week Thirty-Nine:
Set a Daily Intention

"Our intention creates our reality."
—Wayne Dyer

Set a Daily Intention

Often at the beginning of a yoga class or meditation session you are asked to set an intention. Your intention is something that you want to focus on or cultivate throughout your practice. Much like setting an intention before starting your yoga or meditation exercise, it is extremely powerful to set an intention, or focus, for your day.

This week I challenge you to set a daily intention for yourself. When you wake up each morning, check in asking, "How do I want to feel today?" Maybe you want to feel grounded, supported, grateful, or fully present. Write that intention down on a piece of paper to help hold yourself accountable.

Refer to your intention throughout the day and ask yourself, "What can I do to achieve this feeling?" Focus on embodying your desired feeling. If you want to feel abundant, how would someone abundant act? If you want to feel love, how would someone in love act? If this is difficult, reflect on a time when you were experiencing that desired feeling and try reliving that memory.

I love setting intentions in my yoga classes. I have noticed I am more likely to focus on cultivating that intention throughout the class. For instance, if I want to feel grounded, I will pause to notice the ground underneath my feet. If I want to feel present, I will be more deliberate with each stance, not rushing through the poses. I have found the same to be true when I set a daily intention. It always reminds me to be more deliberate in achieving my focus.

Successfully cultivating your desired intention starts by being deliberate with your thoughts and trying to do the things that help evoke that feeling. Always check in at the end of the day to assess whether you accomplished what you set out to do. My hope is that, no matter the degree of success, you find that setting a daily intention brings direction and peace of mind.

Questions to Consider:

- How do I want to feel?

- How does setting a daily intention help me cultivate that feeling?

- What can I do to keep the intention in the forefront of my mind throughout the day?

Week Forty:
Meditate

"Where there is peace and meditation,
there is neither anxiety nor doubt."
—St. Francis of Assisi

Meditate

What if there was a simple practice that could help lower your blood pressure, strengthen your immune system, and increase your ability to concentrate?

That would be sweet, right?

Well, guess what? There is! It is called meditation.

Meditation gives all the above stated health benefits. Most important, meditation helps reduce stress, which has been linked to many major causes of death, sums up science journalist Susan Kuchinskas.[11] Meditation is also a great way to tune in and receive messages from your higher-self and the divine. Although the health benefits of meditation are no secret, not everyone makes time for it.

This week strive to spend at least five to 10 minutes a day meditating. This could be sitting in a quiet place and focusing on your breath, repeating a mantra, watching a candle flicker, or listening to a guided meditation. However you choose to meditate, commit to doing it every day. Check in at the end of each day and take note of any major changes you observe in your mind, body, and spirit.

Having a daily meditation practice has been life-changing for me. I feel more peaceful, connected, and less likely to react negatively in stressful or upsetting situations. I often spend my time meditating to connect to my intuition, Angels and guides, and God for insight.

I have created a free guided meditation, *Enlightened Guidance from Your Guardian Angel*. During this meditation, I help you connect with the presence of your Guardian Angel to receive whatever healing messages need to be heard. To read my blog on the topic and receive your copy of my meditation, visit bit.ly/lcgmmeditation.

You may find that following a guided exercise feels most comfortable when you are new to meditation, but whatever method you prefer, you have so much to gain from this beautiful and inspiring practice.

Questions to Consider:

- What is my favorite way to meditate?

- How do I feel before and after my meditation practice?

- Am I finding myself looking more forward to my meditation sessions as the week goes on?

Week Forty-One:
Keep Learning

"Live as if you were to die tomorrow.
Learn as if you were to live forever."
—*Mahatma Gandhi*

Keep Learning

No matter where you are in your self-love and happiness journey, there will always be new ways to learn and grow. Each of us can greatly benefit from a consistent self-study practice.

Every day this week, commit to spending at least 20 minutes growing your self-study practice from the teachings of today's thought leaders, authors, coaches, and motivational speakers. There is a plethora of ways to learn new information, from reading a book to listening to an audiobook or podcast, and from attending a workshop to signing on to a webinar.

You might be thinking...Really? Twenty minutes? I don't have any time in my schedule!

It is well worth it to find time through creative ways. How about listening to a podcast or YouTube video from your favorite spiritual teacher while you are stuck in traffic, working out, or making dinner? What if you read a self-help book on your phone while you are waiting in line, placed on hold, or on your lunch break?

I never thought I would say this, but I love learning—at least about topics such as self-help, mindset, wealth consciousness, and manifesting. Reading is my favorite way to learn, but I also take courses and classes and often find valuable free audiobooks and lectures on YouTube. I set time in my calendar for learning and have made it part of my daily routine.

Just 20 minutes of learning time a day will add more positivity to your life and have a huge impact on your vibration.

Questions to Consider:

- How do I best learn?

- What kind of learner am I—a reader, a viewer, a listener, or something else?

- How can I best maximize learning in the 20 minutes I have each day?

- Do I feel compelled to share what I am learning with others?

Week Forty-Two:
See for the First Time

"Judgments prevent us from seeing the good that lies beyond appearances."
—Wayne Dyer

See for the First Time

We all have experience with people that, for whatever reason, annoy, anger, or piss us off. In some instances, they evoke feelings of jealousy or resentment. When people trigger fear-based thoughts and emotions within you, it is time to see them again. It is time to see them with love.

In the book *The Universe Has Your Back*, Gabrielle Bernstein challenges her readers to notice when they have detoured from acceptance and love toward judgment and fear. In these moments, it is time to choose a more loving thought.[12]

Gabrielle encourages her readers to pretend we are seeing for the first time those people who get to us. Seeing them without our judgments and preconceived thoughts of who they are. Seeing them as God sees them and as love sees them.

The first time I read this book, I was having a hard time with someone in my life. To be blunt, he was driving me crazy. I went to the park to get some fresh air and read this exercise that found me right at the time I needed it. Seeing this person for the first time allowed me to put aside my judgments and annoyances and really see him. He was craving love as much as I was, and this is what united us. His behavior and neediness was similar to the behaviors I show when I am seeking love and approval from others.

Your ego will try to separate you from others. It attempts to make you think you are better than others or you are less than them. The truth is we are all the same. We all have fears. We all make judgments. We all own parts of ourselves that we try to hide from the outside world.

This week as you notice yourself thinking that your boss is a jerk, your spouse is annoying, or your coworkers are entitled, pause and take a moment. Set aside your judgments, fears, and projections, and see this person for the first time. See this person with love.

Questions to Consider:

- Who triggers fear-based emotions within myself?

- Do I allow differences or unfamiliar qualities in other people to cause fear and judgments?

- How does seeing others for the first time translate to how I react to or interact with them?

- Have I surprised myself or others with my new outlook?

Week Forty-Three:
Get Your Body Moving

"Will is a skill."
—*Jillian Michaels*

Get Your Body Moving

There are many positive benefits to working out, including weight loss, boosted metabolism, and stress reduction. Working out has long been known to help create a healthy body. Did you know there are now study results that indicate that working out can also help create a healthy mind by decreasing depression?

As reported by health and fitness writer Gretchen Reynolds of the *New York Times*, three recent studies have shown that exercise may be an effective treatment for depression and may help to prevent depression as well. One study collected data on over one million men and women who were placed into three groups based on how aerobically fit they were. Those placed in the lowest fitness level were on average 75 percent more likely to be diagnosed with depression than those placed in the greatest fitness level.[13]

So, to help elevate your mood and protect yourself from depression, let's get your body moving!

Here's the challenge. This week I encourage you to spend at least 10 to 15 minutes doing physical exercise every day. Whether you go for a walk; take a yoga, spin, or Pilates class; or follow along with a workout video, choose some form of exercise that motivates and excites you. If you are excited by your exercise of choice, you are much more likely to do it.

If you currently work out, wonderful! This week, push yourself a little harder, work out a little longer, or try out a new routine.

Since college I have consistently tried to work out five to seven days a week. I notice a difference in myself when I don't work out for several days. I seem to be more susceptible to negative thoughts and feel a little less clear-headed and motivated.

I'm fully convinced that exercise can help create a healthier *and* happier you!

Questions to Consider:

- How consistent am I with my work out?

- How are my mind and body affected by working out or not working out?

- How does having a healthier body make me feel about myself?

Week Forty-Four:
Show Thanks

"Trade your expectations for appreciation and your whole world changes in an instant!"
—Tony Robbins

Show Thanks

How often do you express your gratitude to the important people in your life? I am guessing that you do on their birthdays and special holidays and occasions, but what about the rest of the year?

When I ask clients I coach what they are grateful for, a common response is friends and family. When I ask them how often they say "thank you" to their loved ones, a common response is not as often as they should. Yes, it is important to recognize that you are grateful for these special people, but it is just as important that they be properly thanked.

Every day this week I challenge you to tell someone in your life "thank you." Perhaps send a thank you note to your employees or coworkers, write a heartfelt letter to family members, or call your friends and let them know why they are special to you.

Gratitude is such a magnetic feeling and helps you attract more positivity into your life. I have noticed that the more I show love and appreciation for those in my life, the more I get love and appreciation returned to me. At many times in my life I have felt as though I was being ignored or taken advantage of. In those moments, I wanted to give into fear and do the same in return, but I have come to learn that this is my ego making itself known. Fear is not the solution; love, which conquers fear, is.

Imagine how wonderful the world would be if everyone freely gave their thanks and showed just a little more appreciation to one another. What an abundance that would be!

Questions to Consider:

- How often do I let the people in my life know I am thankful for them?

- How will I show thanks to my loved ones this week?

- What bits of information do I know about various loved ones—interests, favorite colors, activities—to help give a special thank you?

Week Forty-Five:
Write Love Letters

"To love oneself is the beginning
of a lifelong romance."
—Oscar Wilde

Write Love Letters

This week's challenge is to show love and appreciation for yourself, this time in the form of love letters.

What do you love and appreciate about yourself? What makes you unique? What reminders or advice would you give yourself when you're having a bad day?

These are all questions to consider when writing your love letters each day this week. You can write one long letter that you add to every day or a separate letter for each day, whatever you feel called to do. Perhaps you hide these letters so you can find them later, or keep them in a safe place to enjoy when you need to be reminded of how extraordinary you are.

I have always loved writing letters and email notes to my significant other. For some reason, I feel it is easier to express myself more deeply through the written word than through the spoken word. For me, it comes naturally to connect with my soul and speak from my heart through writing.

That is exactly what this exercise is about, speaking to yourself from your soul and not your ego. Your soul knows how incredible you are, but your ego will try to fight this truth any chance it gets. If you are still working on getting comfortable with affirmations and mirror work, writing is another effective way to express those important words that you need to receive from yourself.

So grab a pen, connect with your soul, and start writing! Let your self-love lead the way...

Questions to Consider:

- What comes up for me when I think about writing myself a love letter?

- What does my soul need to hear?

- How do I describe my ideal love letter—scented, on quality stationery, decorated with thoughtful embellishments, or written in deliberate handwriting or lettering?

- What can I do to make my love letters into special keepsakes?

Week Forty-Six:
Give a Little More

"The heart that gives, gathers."
—Tao Te Ching

Give a Little More

Have you ever experienced a great sense of joy when giving to others? Do you experience that same level of joy when you give to yourself?

As Miami University psychology professor Allen McConnell posted on the *Psychology Today* blog, research conducted on over 600 Americans showed that those who experience a greater sense of happiness spend more money on others than on themselves. This pattern was found across all surveyed income levels.[14]

Additional study results, reported by *Cleveland Clinic* magazine contributor and psychologist Scott Bea, support that there are several health benefits associated with giving back. These benefits include lowered blood pressure and stress levels, increased self-esteem, and greater happiness.[15] Wow, giving back really gives back!

This week think about how you can give a little more. Can you increase your donation to your favorite charity by a few dollars? Is there someone in your life you can surprise with a much-needed gift? If money is an issue, consider other ways you can give, perhaps by donating more time to a good cause or sending a letter to the troops or someone else in need of a smile.

My parents have always joked with me that I have never been able to pass up a Salvation Army bucket. Since childhood, I have always loved giving money to those in need. Whenever I saw those red buckets, I had to stop, even if I had only a few cents to give. Because giving brings me so much joy and fulfillment, I was not surprised to learn of the research that proves this point.

When you give, you truly receive.

Questions to Consider:

- How does how I feel when I give to others compare to how I feel when I give to myself?

- For the charities that I already give to, how much more can I give this week?

- Besides money, what gifts can I offer this week?

- Which community organizations need volunteers this week?

Week Forty-Seven:
Really Listen

"Most people do not listen with the intent to understand; they listen with the intent to reply."
—Stephen Covey

Really Listen

Sometimes we are "hearing" other people, but we may not be truly "listening" to what they are saying. Our first instinct is often to share wins, dominate the conversation, or get in the last word instead of intentionally participating, particularly when others are speaking. This week is all about approaching your conversations differently and being fully engaged.

When you are engaged in conversation, make a conscious effort to be fully present. Put away your phone, turn off the TV, stop daydreaming, and practice active listening, or fully listening and engaging without distractions, to what is being said.

What new things can you learn and discover about your friends, family, and coworkers by actively listening to what they are sharing with you? How can you deepen your relationships by being fully invested in what your loved ones are saying? The more you take interest in what others share of themselves, the more loved they will feel, and the more love you will receive.

Ironically enough, as listening is a big part of being a life coach, I was not always a good listener. In fact, I once took a quiz at a networking event that showed I was a below-average active listener. I found this quite upsetting because I didn't want the people in my life to think I found what they said to be uninteresting or unimportant.

To this day, I do catch myself looking down at my phone when out with friends, or watching the TV when my loved ones are trying to talk to me. I try to break these habits because I understand that the more I fully engage with those in my life, the more connected to them I feel.

This week come to each conversation with open ears and an open heart, ready to listen.

Questions to Consider:

- Do I find myself talking more than listening?

- Am I often working on my next response while the other person is still talking?

- Do I ask questions about a topic only to find out the information has already been covered?

Week Forty-Eight:
Make Others Feel Remembered

"I've learned that people will forget what you said, people will forget what you did, but people will never forget how you made them feel."
—Maya Angelou

Make Others Feel Remembered

Do you know someone who has recently lost a loved one and is experiencing a lot of pain? Is a family member unable to make it to family gatherings because of conflicting work hours or a lack of transportation? Have you noticed your elderly neighbors haven't had any visitors recently?

The challenge this week is to show kindness to people who may feel forgotten or left out. What can you do to make them feel remembered and loved? Perhaps you stop by for a visit, send a card, make a call, help at a local shelter, or donate gifts to a family in need. Be genuine in making them feel special and showing them someone cares.

When my mom shares with me touching stories about the people in need that her church helps, many of them share one significant common factor—how truly touched they are when they feel remembered. Many of these people cannot pay their bills, don't know where their next meal will come from, or are doubtful if they will be able to supply their children the basic needs. When someone donates money, brings in clothes or food, or simply provides an ear to listen, it truly touches their lives and often brings them to tears of gratitude.

One of the most beautiful and blessed gifts you can give is remembering someone who feels forgotten. One small act of kindness can truly change many lives for the better, including your own.

Questions to Consider:

- What organizations that serve the forgotten could I spend time visiting?

- Who do I know that might be lonely or feel forgotten?

- How can I make them feel remembered this week?

Week Forty-Nine:
Go to Bed Happy

"As a well-spent day brings happy sleep..."
—*Leonardo da Vinci*

Go to Bed Happy

In the song "Mad," Ne-Yo sings, "I don't wanna go to bed mad at you, and I don't want you to go to bed mad at me." This song holds an important lesson: Don't go to bed mad! If you do, chances are you will wake up feeling the same way. As you learned earlier in this book, our reality is a response to the thoughts we think and the emotions we feel. This idea is the law of attraction at work.

If you are feeling mad or upset, say a prayer that calms you before going to sleep. If you have had an argument with someone, agree to disagree and make peace until the morning when you can talk about the situation with a clear head.

If you find it difficult to set things right before bedtime, know that you are never alone and you do not have to rely on your own strength. Ask the divine to help you see the person or situation with love. Meditate to release your anger and negativity, and journal if need be.

Before bed, I do a nightly ritual. I read my affirmations, visualize the life I want to create, meditate, and thank God for the day. My ritual helps to release any negativity that I experienced that day and go to bed happy. And when I go to bed happy, I usually wake up in the same state.

Tomorrow is indeed another day.

Questions to Consider:

- Am I deliberate about how I feel before going to bed?

- Do I feel hopeful about tomorrow, even after a day filled with negativity?

- What can I do to go to bed happy this week?

Week Fifty:
Notice the Abundance Around You

"When you focus on what you have,
your abundance increases."
—Oprah Winfrey

Notice the Abundance Around You

Do you often find yourself in a state of lack? Do you repeatedly think or say you never have enough? Do you worry or stress about your financial situation?

If you constantly think or say that you never have enough, you will create a reality where you never have enough. If you focus on the abundance all around you, you will attract more abundance.

This week notice and write down everything you receive. Write down any money paid to you, the amounts from your paychecks and gift cards, and any change you find lying on the floor or in the street. If someone gives you a gift or you win a prize or award, write that down along with their estimated cash value.

Money mindset mentor Denise Duffield-Thomas is a big advocate of tracking everything you receive.[16] I started doing this exercise daily after reading her book *Get Rich, Lucky Bitch*, and it never ceases to amaze me how much I receive! There have been days when I have received several thousands of dollars' worth of unexpected gifts— baskets, raffled items, trips, hotel stays, and coaching programs. My clients and I have also been the lucky recipients of (unforeseen) checks, money, and prizes.

As the week goes on, continue to take note of your abundance. Anytime you write down something new, give thanks to the Universe. The more you acknowledge and show thanks, the more will come to you.

Questions to Consider:

- What are my dominant thoughts about my finances?

- Do I celebrate all the money and gifts that come my way?

- Do I keep a record of how my abundance goes back out into the world?

Week Fifty-One:
Make Sleep a Priority

*"Sleep is that golden chain that binds health
and our bodies together."*
—*Thomas Dekker*

Make Sleep a Priority

Do you find yourself staying up late to watch one more episode of your favorite Netflix or Hulu show? Do you procrastinate during the day only to find motivation right before bedtime? Do you hit snooze more times than you would like to admit? Observe your answers without judgment while noting that your responses could all be signs that you are not making sleep a priority in your life.

As fitness and health expert Alyssa Sparacino shared in *Health* magazine, a full night's sleep can result in a wide variety of benefits: improved memory, increases in creativity and emotional stability, sharpened attention levels, and decreased stress and anxiety.[17] I certainly can attest to my missing out on all the above when I've failed to get enough rest—I am not fun to be around!

This week, as often as possible, try to get a full night's sleep. Turn off the television before being tempted to watch just one more episode that would cause you to go to bed late. Strive to be productive during the day so you aren't up until the wee hours working to get things done. If you get good sleep, you are more likely to get up the first time your alarm goes off, prepared to seize the day!

Questions to Consider:

- Do I make sleep a priority?

- What or who do I make more important than sleep?

- How do my body and mind feel because of these choices?

Week Fifty-Two:
Just Breathe

*"Breathing in, I calm my body. Breathing out,
I smile. Dwelling in the present moment,
I know this is a wonderful moment."*
—Thich Nhat Hanh

Just Breathe

Pranayama, or breathing, is one of the basic functions of your body. Because breathing is a given with life, we normally do not give it much thought. Besides during yoga and meditation, how often do you focus on your breathing?

This week breathing is the solution when fear, doubt, anger, uncertainty, or any other low-vibrational thoughts surface. Before making any big decisions, saying something you might regret, or acting in fear, simply allow yourself to breathe. Close your eyes and focus on your breath for 15 seconds or more before acting.

Focusing on your breath allows you to be present first. When you take these moments to pause and connect with your breath, you are more likely to act from a place of love than a place of fear.

Throughout my teens and early twenties, I was very quick to react. I would find myself saying and doing things I regretted because I acted out of fear. Connecting with my breath allows me to have time for love to come in and fill my heart. Do I always remember to connect with my breath and pause? No, of course not. But I do it much more than I did several years ago, and that is certainly worth celebrating.

Questions to Consider:

- How often do I focus on my breath?

- Do I allow myself to breathe before acting in moments of stress?

- How does my mood change when I focus on my breath?

Conclusion

First, congratulations!!! I am beyond proud of you for completing the weekly challenges in this book and making your own self-love and happiness a priority.

Second, if you were overly hard on yourself throughout any of the challenges or if you were experiencing resistance, I want to reassure you it is okay! These challenges most likely pushed you out of your comfort zone, and your brain naturally resisted change for safety's sake. As one of my clients stated perfectly, you should strive for progress, not perfection.

After reading and implementing these 52 challenges, I hope that you can see firsthand that happiness is a choice. It is your choice, and no one can take that away from you. I hope you now realize that you don't have to wait for your circumstances to improve to be happy. When you are happy and high vibrational your circumstances will improve, not the other way around. You also don't have to search for happiness because you can decide to be happy at any time. Your soul is always ready. It is your ego that wants you to believe that you need to search for happiness outside of yourself.

If you have felt or are feeling how I was a few years ago, lost and unhappy, looking for more out of life, I feel for you. I know that in those moments the pain can feel very real. It can feel like the weight of the world is on your shoulders, as though it will never get easier. I want to let you know that it can and will. You have the power to make it happen. As Robert Holden stated, "Happiness is only ever one thought away at most." Commit to choosing happiness and continue doing the things that bring you closer to joy every single day.

As I mentioned in the beginning of this book, implementing the principles of these challenges changed my life. I went from being single or in unhealthy relationships to finding my soulmate and getting engaged. I doubled my income in a year and found my dream job after being passed up for four promotions, leaving a job, and being unemployed. I moved to my dream apartment in Venice with an ocean view after longing to live near the beach for years. I have built a business and made it my full-time job in a few short months. I went from feeling lost and unhappy to finding a deeper level of happiness and self-love than I ever could have imagined.

I did not commit to doing the principles in this book to never think about them again. I did and continue to do them regularly. I showed up to my life, and I am doing the work to create the life I truly desire.

As humans, we will never be perfect, nor should we strive to be. What we should strive for is to be a better version of ourselves than we were yesterday. These challenges help us do exactly that. They teach happiness, self-love, positivity, gratitude, self-care, and ways to connect with our joy.

My challenge to you is to continue to implement these challenges and everyday commit to choosing a life filled with happiness and love.

Looking for More?

If you have not yet created the happiness or fulfillment you are desiring or if you are looking to take your happiness journey to the next level, I encourage you to seek out a teacher, mentor, or coach who you connect with.

As a Buddhist Proverb said: "When the student is ready, the teacher will appear."

I don't want you wasting another day feeling stuck, not living the life that you desire, and not fulfilling your dreams. My life changed the day I decided that getting by each day was *not* good enough anymore. By investing in myself and hiring my own life coach, I transformed every major aspect of my life. I want that for you, too.

My personal journey to find happiness and self-love is what inspired me to become a life coach. I am thrilled to share what I have learned with powerhouse women like you, who are ready to up-level their lives and make serious positive changes.

If you are ready to make a life-changing transformation and claim a life filled with abundance, happiness, and self-love, check out lifecoachgingermarie.com/coaching. There you will find in-depth information about my one-on-one coaching programs, and you can apply for a clarity call to see if working together would be a good fit.

I am so proud of you for completing my weekly challenges!

With Love,

Ginger Marie

References

1. Happiness. (accessed February 10, 2017). In *Dictionary.com*. Retrieved from http://dictionary.com/happiness

2. Williams, R. (2010, August 21). Why "stretch goals" are a waste of time. *Psychology Today*. Retrieved from https://www.psychologytoday.com/blog/wired-success/201008/why-stretch-goals-are-waste-time

3. Holden, R. (2009). *Be happy: Release the power of happiness in you* (p. 36). Carlsbad, CA: Hay House.

4. Hay, L. (no date). *What is mirror work?* Retrieved from http://www.louisehay.com/what-is-mirror-work/

5. Holden, R. (no date). *What is mirror work? An introduction to Louise Hay's famous exercise.* Retrieved from http://www.robertholden.org/blog/tag/mirror-work/

6. Lechner, T. (no date). *6 reasons why laughter is the best medicine.* Retrieved from The Chopra Center website: http://www.chopra.com/articles/6-reasons-why-laughter-is-the-best-medicine

7. Holden, R. (no date). *Where do you rank on the forgiveness scale? Learn how to score yourself and transform your relationship with yourself and everyone.* Retrieved from http://www.robertholden.org/blog/rank-forgiveness-scale/

8. Dooley, R. (2013, February 26). Why faking a smile is a good thing. *Forbes*. Retrieved from http://www.forbes.com/sites/rogerdooley/2013/02/26/fake-smile/#321201b3334c

9. Wise, A. (2014, July 18). Here's proof going outside makes you healthier. *The Huffington Post*. Retrieved from http://www.huffingtonpost.com/2014/06/22/how-the-outdoors-make-you_n_5508964.html

10. Govender, S. (no date). *Is crying good for you?* Retrieved from the WebMD website: http://www.webmd.com/balance/features/is-crying-good-for-you#1

11. Kuchinskas, S. (no date). *Meditation heals body and mind*. Retrieved from the WebMD website: http://www.webmd.com/balance/features/meditation-heals-body-and-mind#1

12. Bernstein, G. (2016). *The universe has your back: Transform fear to faith* (pp. 135-6). Carlsbad, CA: Hay House.

13. Reynolds, G. (2016, November 16). How exercise might keep depression at bay. *The New York Times*. Retrieved from https://www.nytimes.com/2016/11/16/well/move/how-exercise-might-keep-depression-at-bay.html?_r=0

14. McConnell, A. R. (2010, December 25). Giving really is better than receiving. *Psychology Today*. Retrieved from https://www.psychologytoday.com/blog/the-social-self/201012/giving-really-is-better-receiving

15. Bea, S. (no date). *Wanna give? This is your brain on a 'helper's high.'* Retrieved from The Cleveland Clinic website: https://health.clevelandclinic.org/2016/11/why-giving-is-good-for-your-health/

16. Duffield-Thomas, D. (2013). *Get rich, lucky bitch: Release your money blocks and live a first class life*. Author.

17. Sparacino, A. (no date). 11 surprising health benefits of sleep. *Health*. Retrieved from health.com/health/gallery/0,20459221,00.html#steer-clear-of-depression-0

About the Author

Ginger Marie Corwin is a Life Coach, Angel Card Reader, and Yoga Teacher. She helps women who are searching for a deeper level of happiness and self-love to find self-acceptance, power in thoughts, and happiness in the present moment, so that they can feel financially free, fiercely confident, and in control of their lives.

Ginger Marie trained under *New York Times* best-selling author and founder of the Happiness Project, Robert Holden, Ph.D., where she received her Coach Camp Certification. Ginger is a Certified Angel Card Reader™ and offers private clients Angel Card Readings. She recently finished her 200-hour Yoga Teacher Training from YogaWorks and currently teaches yoga in Claremont, CA.

Ginger Marie is originally from Cleveland, Ohio, and has two brothers and a sister. She lives in the suburbs of Los Angeles, is engaged, and will marry her fiancé, Nic, in November of 2017.

Visit the author online at lifecoachgingermarie.com.

Made in the USA
San Bernardino,
CA